Price Action Trends Trading

Mastering trading trends, Resistance and support

Lewis Wood

This book Price Action Trading is committed to each forex dealer and furthermore for fledgling brokers and amateurs who are keen on learning and trading the forex market including old merchants too with almost no experience, taking the necessary steps to win in forex trading, rather than giving reasons.

Table of content

Introduction

Price action trading is a procedure for monetary market hypothesis which comprises of the investigation of fundamental cost development across time. It's utilized by many retail merchants and frequently by institutional brokers and multifaceted investments directors to make forecasts on the future heading of the cost of a security or monetary market.

Set forth plainly, cost activity is the way cost changes, i.e., the 'activity' of cost. It's most effortlessly seen in business sectors with high liquidity and unpredictability, however whatever is traded in an unregulated economy will create cost activity.

Cost activity exchanging overlooks the central factors that impact a market's development, and on second thought it checks out principally at the market's cost history, in other words its cost development across a time frame. Hence, cost activity is a structure a specialized investigation, however what separates it from most types of specialized examination is that its fundamental spotlight is on the relationship of a market's ongoing cost to its past or late costs, rather than 'second-hand' esteems that are gotten from that cost history.

As such, cost activity exchanging is a 'unadulterated' type of specialized investigation since it incorporates no second-hand, cost determined markers. Cost activity dealers are exclusively worried about the direct information a market creates about itself; it's cost development over the long run.

Chapter 1

What is price action in trading?

Price action in trading analyses the exhibition of a security, file, product or money to foresee what it could do from here on out. Assuming that your cost activity investigation lets you know that the cost is going to rise, you should take a long position, or on the other hand on the off chance that you accept that the cost will fall, you could decide to short the resource.

Understanding cost activity exchanging includes taking a gander at designs and distinguishing the key pointers that could affect your ventures. There are various different cost activity strategies that numerous merchants use to foresee market developments and make transient increases.

What do 'pure' or 'naked' price action mean?

Naked price action - otherwise called unadulterated cost activity - implies that you are making your exchanges dependent exclusively upon the costs that you can see before you. It's similar to driving with your sat nav switched off. Rather than depending on complex equations and tedious investigation, you make your exchanges utilizing your comprehension own might interpret the market.

What are price action signals?

Cost activity signals - some of the time called cost activity examples, or cost activity triggers - are effectively conspicuous examples in a market, which can be utilized to foresee future market conduct. Experienced merchants can in some cases spot these signs initially by perceiving specific shapes or reiterations in past execution.

Price action vs indicators vs technical analysis: what is the difference?

Price action indicators are glimmers of action on an exchanging graph that signal the development of a pattern. Prepared merchants can recognize these pointers rapidly and use them to make informed wagers available progressively.

Specialized examination utilizes a scope of various computations to foresee future cost developments. Paradoxically, cost activity depends just on the value developments of a resource inside your exchanging time period.

As it were, technical analysis is attempting to track down request inside the apparently tumultuous universe of exchanging, while cost activity permits the dealer to take a more customary stomach based exchanging approach by spotting cost activity pointers and following up on them.

Price action vs indicators vs technical analysis: what is the difference?

On a trading chart, price action indicators are glimmers of activity that indicate the onset of a trend. Experienced traders are able to quickly identify these indicators and use them to make informed real-time bets on the market.

To predict how prices will change in the future, technical analysis uses a variety of different calculations. Price action, on the other hand, is solely dependent on an asset's price movements within your trading time frame.

Price action allows traders to take a more conventional gut-based trading approach by spotting price action indicators and acting on them, whereas technical analysis is trying to find order in the seemingly chaotic world of trading.

Why is price action popular among forex traders?

The forex market is particularly popular with price action traders for a few reasons.

Because it is so liquid, traders may find it easier to quickly open and close positions. The forex market is always changing, but it rarely experiences significant highs or lows. The market's maturity makes it easier to spot recurring patterns and trends, making it ideal for novice traders who wish to experiment with smaller trades before scaling up as their expertise grows.

How to trade using price action: tips to get started

To start price action trading, just follow these six steps:

1. Create an account or log in
2. Identify the market you want to trade
3. Build a personalised trading plan
4. Decide whether to go long or short
5. Open and monitor your position

Top seven trading strategies with price action signals

1. Price action trend trading
2. Pin bar
3. Inside bar
4. Trend following retracement entry
5. Trend following breakout entry
6. Head and shoulders reversal trade
7. The sequence of highs and lows

Price action trend trading

if price action trading is the study of price movements, price action trend trading is the study of trends. Traders can make use of a number of trading techniques to spot and follow price action trends such as the head and shoulders trade reversal.

By following price action trends as soon as they become apparent, this is an excellent trading tool for novice traders because it enables them to effectively learn from their more experienced peers. You would open a "buy" position to profit from the green uptrends, or a "sell" position to profit from the red downtrends, as shown in the screenshot below.

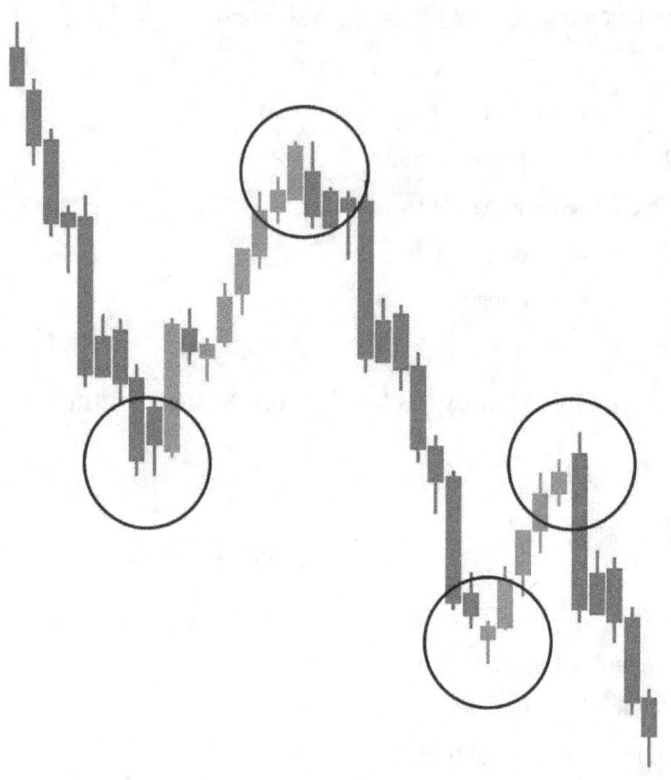

The pin Bar

The pin bar pattern looks like a candle with a long wick on it, which is why it is sometimes called the candlestick strategy. The "wick" or tail depicts the price range that was rejected, indicating a sharp reversal and rejection of a particular price.

To decide whether to take a long or short position in the market, traders will make the assumption that the price will continue to move in the opposite direction to the tail. For instance, if the lower tail of the pin bar pattern is long, it indicates to the trader that lower prices have been rejected in the past, indicating that the price may soon rise.

Chapter 2

Inside bar

Within bar design is a two-bar procedure, where the internal bar is more modest than the external bar, and falls inside the high and low scope of the external bar (or mother bar). Inside bars typically form during a period of market consolidation, but they can also serve as a red herring, indicating a market pivot.

This trend can be seen at a glance by skilled traders, who should be able to use their macro knowledge to determine whether the inside bar is a consolidation or a change in the current trend. The likelihood of a price rising or falling is determined by the inside bar's size and position.

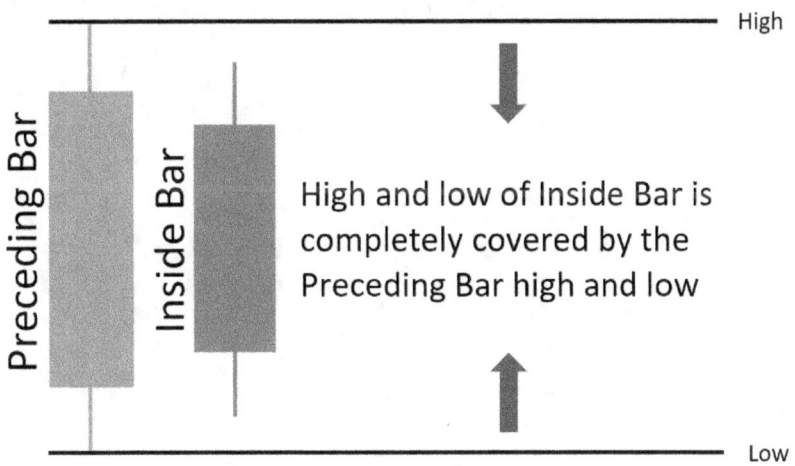

Trend following retracement entry

This is a relatively simple price action strategy whereby the trader simply follows the existing trend.

If a price is on a clear downturn, with lower highs being consistently created, the trader might look to take a short position. If prices are rising incrementally, with the highs and lows trending increasingly higher, then the trader might want to buy in.

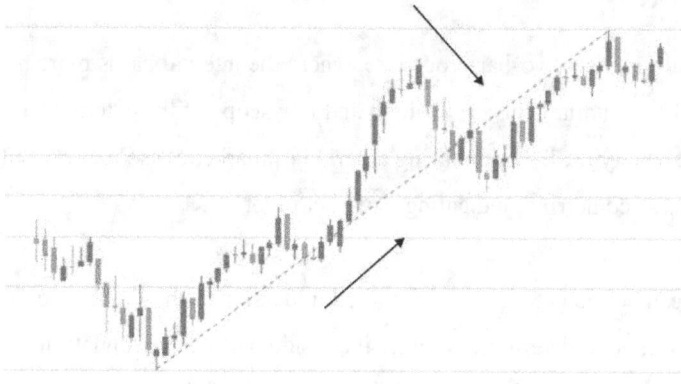

Trend following breakout entry

This trend anticipates a retracement following a price spike and tracks any significant market movements. A breakout occurs when a market moves outside of a clearly defined support or resistance line.

If the stock moves above the resistance line or is trending upward, traders can take a long position and use this as a signal to act. If the stock moves below the support line, traders can take a short position.

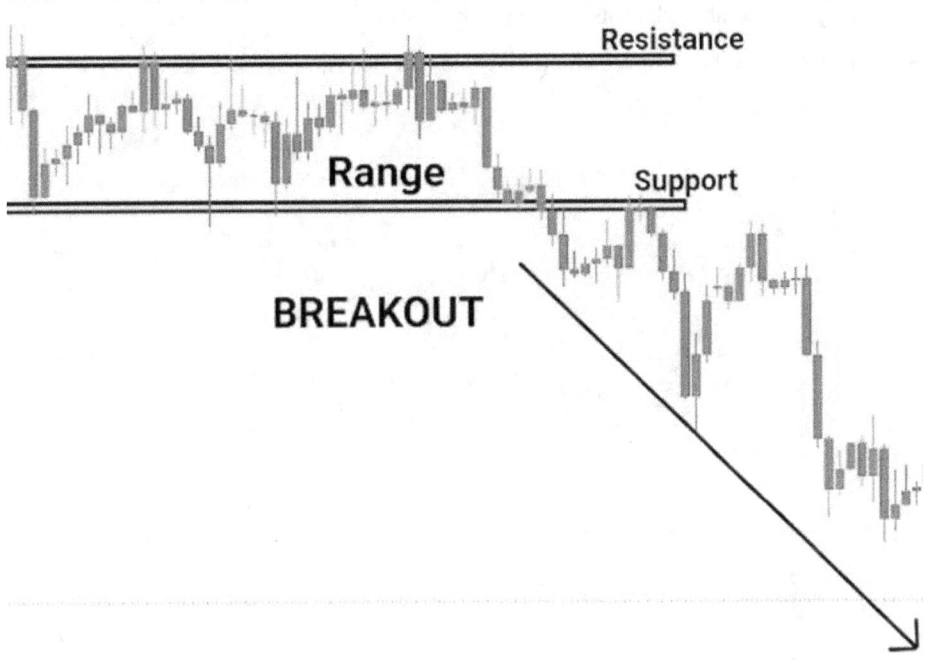

Head and shoulders inversion exchange

As the name proposes, the head and shoulders design is a market development that seems to be the outline of a head and shoulders. At the end of the day, costs rise, fall, rise significantly further, fall once more, and ascend to a lower high before a humble drop.

The head and shoulders inversion exchange is one of the most famous cost activity exchanging systems as it's somewhat simple to pick a section point (by and large just after the principal shoulder) and to set a stop misfortune (after the subsequent shoulder) to exploit an impermanent pinnacle (the head).

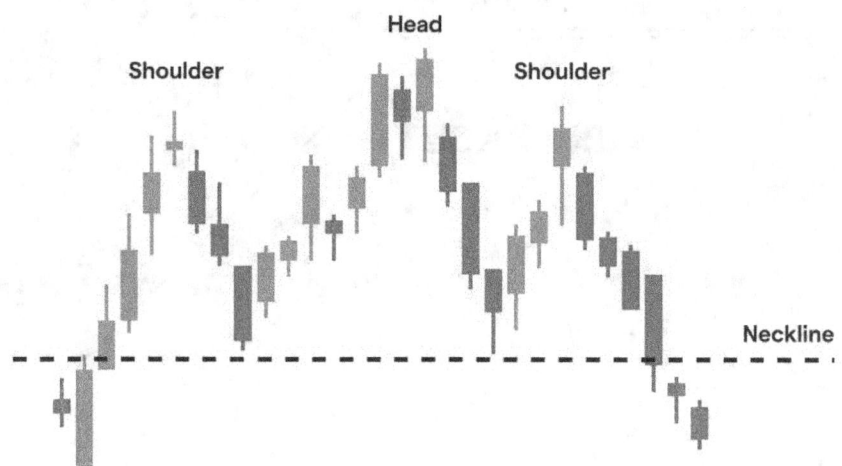

The sequence of highs and lows

At its center, cost activity exchanging is a round of ups and downs. Cost activity dealers can follow the arrangement of ups and downs procedure to outline arising patterns in their market.

For instance, assuming a cost is exchanging at new records all around, this shows that it's on a vertical pattern. Assuming it's exchanging at worse high points and lows, it's moving downwards. Dealers can utilize their insight into the grouping of ups and downs to pick a passage point at the lower end of a vertical pattern, and by setting a stop not long before the past higher low.

Chapter 3

Markets For Price Action Trading

Price action analysis focuses on pattern recognition. Hence, it works in most actively traded markets, as long as reliable price data is available. This is one of the advantages of technical analysis methods.

Generally, price action traders favor the forex, futures, stock market, and even the cryptocurrency market.

Here are more examples of analyzing price action in a variety of markets:

Stocks

Futures

Forex

Cryptocurrency

The optimal approach selects markets that have sufficient liquidity and volatility. These characteristics allow better expression of price patterns and reasonable execution of trades.

Essential Price Action Trading Concepts

For trading with price action, there are a few essential building blocks.

1. Price Patterns
2. Market Swings
3. Support and Resistance
4. Trend Lines and Channels

This section will introduce them together with ample resources to learn more.

1. Price Patterns

There are many cost designs including both present moment and long haul designs.

Given the legitimate market setting, these examples offer exchanging open doors, otherwise called exchanging arrangements.

These are some popular price patterns:

Hikkake
Engulfing Candlestick
Inside Bar

We also have comprehensive reference lists of common price patterns:

Bar Patterns
Candlestick Patterns
Chart Patterns

2. Market Swings

The market moves in swings. Hence, the zigzag movement forms the basic structure of the market.

Price action trading interprets higher highs and higher lows as an uptrend and lower highs and lower lows as a downtrend.

Interpreting market swings probably won't be instinctive from the outset. Provided that this is true, moving midpoints can be an important device for explaining market swings. Allude to this aide for more data.

At last, an eminent structure on the way of behaving of market swings is the Elliot Wave Hypothesis, which hypothesizes a 8-wave design as a fractal of market development. While it endeavors to frame a thorough hypothesis, reasonable execution is precarious.

3. Support & Resistance

Support regions are probably going to dismiss value upwards, and opposition regions keep the market from transcending it. They are basic ideas for cost activity exchanging.

Brokers project backing and obstruction levels utilizing swing turn focuses and other cost developments like blockage.

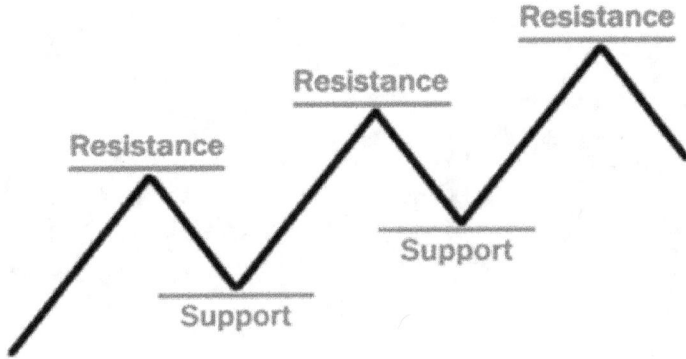

Support and resistance are core price action concepts. Therefore, the key to success is finding adequate support and resistance areas.

4. Trend Lines & Channels

Pattern lines interface swing turns to follow patterns and act as help and opposition.

In a bull pattern, pattern lines are drawn by associating turn lows. In a bear pattern, pattern lines are drawn with turn highs.

By broadening an equal line from the pattern line, we can frame an accommodating exchanging channel for expecting backing and obstruction regions.

The diagram underneath shows a model.

Chapter 4

Price Action Trading Methods

Most price action trading strategies combine price patterns with support and resistance areas.

The standard approach involves looking for:

A bullish price pattern at a support area for a long trade; or
A bearish price pattern at a resistance area for a short trade.
You can entirely rely on price action analysis or incorporate other tools to support it.

1. Pure Price Action

Some traders use price action analysis exclusively. They take on a moderate methodology and put no pointers on their diagrams.

These dealers normally utilize optional procedures and are knowledgeable in spotting value examples and backing/opposition regions.

2. Price Action With Volume

Review the Dow Hypothesis we talked about above?

One more principle of the Dow Hypothesis is that volume ought to increment in the pattern heading and diminishing while moving against it.

Consequently, it isn't is business as usual that volume investigation is a standard supplement to cost activity exchanging. Old style volume examination consolidates volume designs with outline examples to assess an exchanging an open door.

Incorporating volume with cost activity has likewise prompted the improvement of Volume Spread Investigation, which depends on Richard Wyckoff's work on the connection among volume and the spread (scope) of the bar.

Observing price action with volume leads to intriguing trading methods. However, I recommend including volume only after familiarizing yourself with price action.

3. Price Action With Indicators

Notwithstanding the accentuation on cost examination, numerous dealers actually track down esteem in pointers.

The most famous exchanging pointer among cost activity merchants is the moving normal. It fills in as a pattern marker and a unique help/obstruction all the while.

A model is Al Creeks' exchanging approach which utilizes a 20-period remarkable moving normal. The outline underneath shows this technique in real life.

In Steve Nison's books on candlesticks, he also discussed how to analyze candlestick patterns with trading indicators. If you are interested in this approach, refer to the articles below:

Trading Candlestick Patterns With The RSI
Swing Trading Candlesticks With Stochastic
Candlestick Pattern With A Moving Average

4. Beyond The Primer

You've just completed a short introductory guide to price action.

What lies beyond?

This is what I recommend. In sequence, learn how to:

Describe the market in terms of price action features

Analyze what the market is doing right now

Select trading setups

Most traders bounce directly into tracking down exchange arrangements. Yet, over the long haul, this strategy will misfire as you pass up building a strong groundwork.

The most ideal way to learn is to notice and concentrate on cost developments yourself. So load up your outlines, and begin following through on more regard for cost, the most pivotal variable.

Chapter 5

Support And Resistance

Support and resistance underlies the main cost activity exchanging ideas. You can turn into a capable broker in the event that you ace help and obstruction.

The idea of help and obstruction is a foundation of cost activity exchanging. A colossal piece of cost activity exchanging relates to breaking down help and obstruction levels of various degrees. The point is to coordinate them to shape your market assessment and execute your exchanges.

In this aide, you'll learn all that you need to be familiar with help and opposition - from hypothesis and specialized rules, to muddled contemplations.

Defining Support and Resistance

To begin with, what is backing and opposition (S/R)?

Basically, they are value levels (or regions) where brokers expect that a shift in market course is more probable than irregular.

This definition is imperative to the job S/R plays in making an exchanging edge.

In the event that our perspective available is altogether and for all time irregular, it is basically impossible to benefit from the market. Notwithstanding, when we see an inclination for the market to act somehow, exchanging open doors introduce themselves.

A support level is an obstacle to falling prices.

It goes about as a cost floor as long as it stays powerful. At the point when the market floats towards a help level, we expect that the market has a more than irregular possibility being ended at that level.

A resistance level is a barrier to rising prices.

It goes about as a cost roof while it is powerful. At the point when the market ascends towards an opposition level, we expect that the market will have a more than irregular possibility halting its climb.

Before we continue on, how about we move one point.

It is urgent to perceive that help and obstruction levels are zones. Accuracy is an extravagance in the probabilistic market. Utilizing cost ranges (zones) rather than accurate cost levels mirror this comprehension.

(Typically, I draw the support and resistance zones around the shadows of the candlesticks to project a zone.)

How to mark a support or resistance level

We can group the methods under the following labels:

Market Structure Projection

Projected With Computation

Price Action Formations

Volume Formations

Computed Levels

Psychological Levels

This part will examine market structure projection more meticulously and give a concise outline of the other S/R types.

(Every strategy merits a different aide whenever examined exhaustively. Furthermore, I desire to ultimately make individual aides for them. For the time being, I'll show them and connection them to pertinent assets tracked down on or off our site.)

1. Market Structure Projection

Look at any price chart, and you will see peaks and troughs. Trades call these turning points swing pivots.

The chart below highlights the market swings with the help of a color-coded Hull Moving Average.

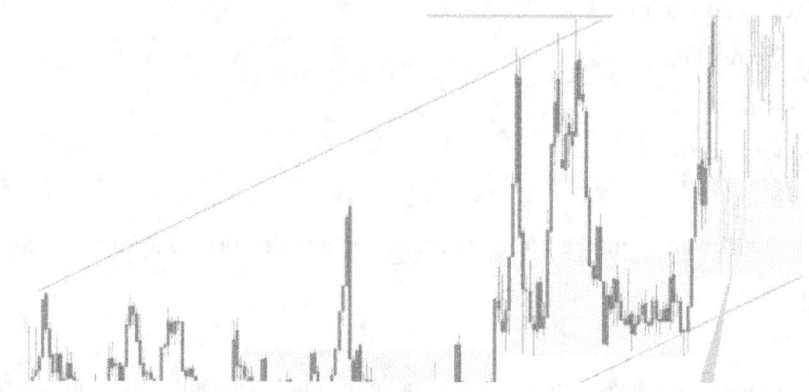

Peaks are swing highs. Troughs are swing lows.

Together, the peaks and troughs form the fundamental market structure.

If you are new to price action trading, you should spend your time on market structure type S/Rs. Doing so will help build a solid foundation for understanding price action.

There are three main ways to project support and resistance from the market structure:

Projecting a horizontal line from one or more swing pivot (Horizontal S/R)
Connecting two swing highs and casting the resulting line (Trendline or Channel Trendline)

Connecting two swing lows and casting the resultant line (Trendline or Channel Trendline

(These lines additionally structure the reason for the whole arrangement of graph designs like the Bull Banner and the Head and Shoulders.)

As may be obvious, every one of the techniques include picking a swing turn (or defining moment) as an anchor and extending a line to one side of the graph.

The graph underneath shows instances of the various sorts of help and obstruction you can project from the market structure.

The horizontal levels projected from the swing pivots are the most basic form of S/R.

Subsequently, they will shape the pillar of our conversations beneath. They work well for to represent the major rules that apply extensively to a wide range of help and opposition.

Chapter 6

2. Projected With Calculation

Like the market structure techniques covered over, these S/R levels require picking a cost anchor.

Yet, in addition, they involve some basic calculation.

Fibonacci Retracements and Extensions (The Golden Ratio)

Andrews' Pitchfork (A simple 50% ratio)

Speed-lines (Simple fractions)

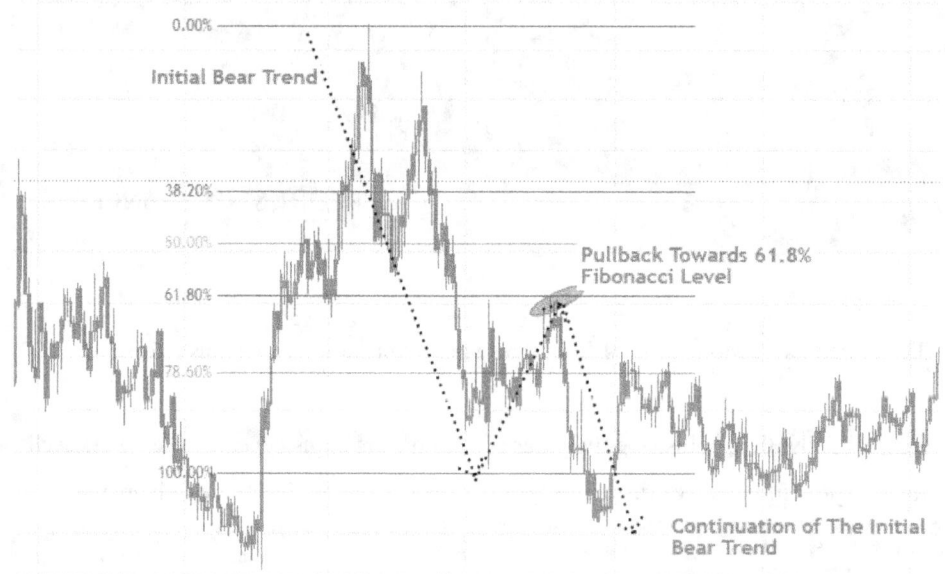

3. Price Action Formation

Price action formations offer a reliable and no-fuss method to mark S/R zones.

After learning how to project S/R from the market structure, focusing on price action formations is the natural progression.

Price Gaps

Congestion Zones

Measured Moves

4. Volume Formations

Volume represents market interest, and this interest manifests as significant S/R levels.

Extreme or concentrated volume are reliable signals.

Climactic Volume - candlestick chart, range bar chart

Market Profile

Price by Volume

VWAP

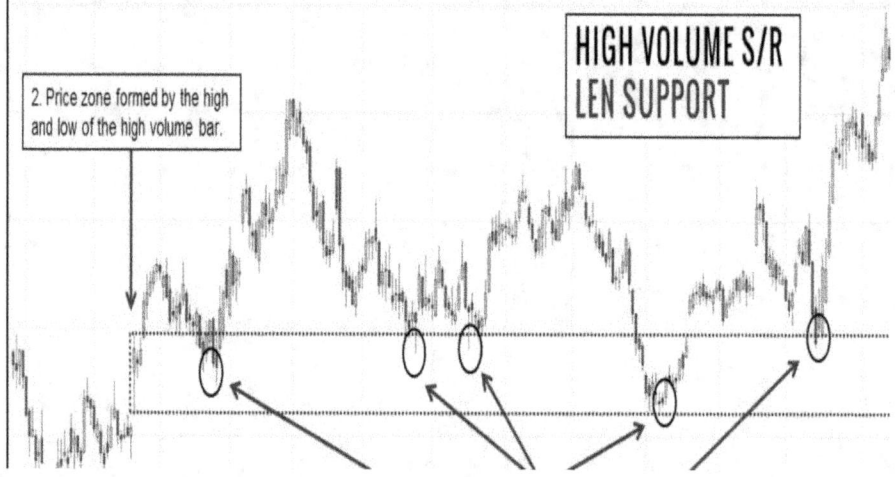

5. Computed Levels

You can also use indicators that overlay price action as S/R zones.

There are endless options here, and we are listing a subset.

Moving averages

Volatility bands - Bollinger and Keltner

Calculated pivots - Floor Traders, Camarilla, Woodies

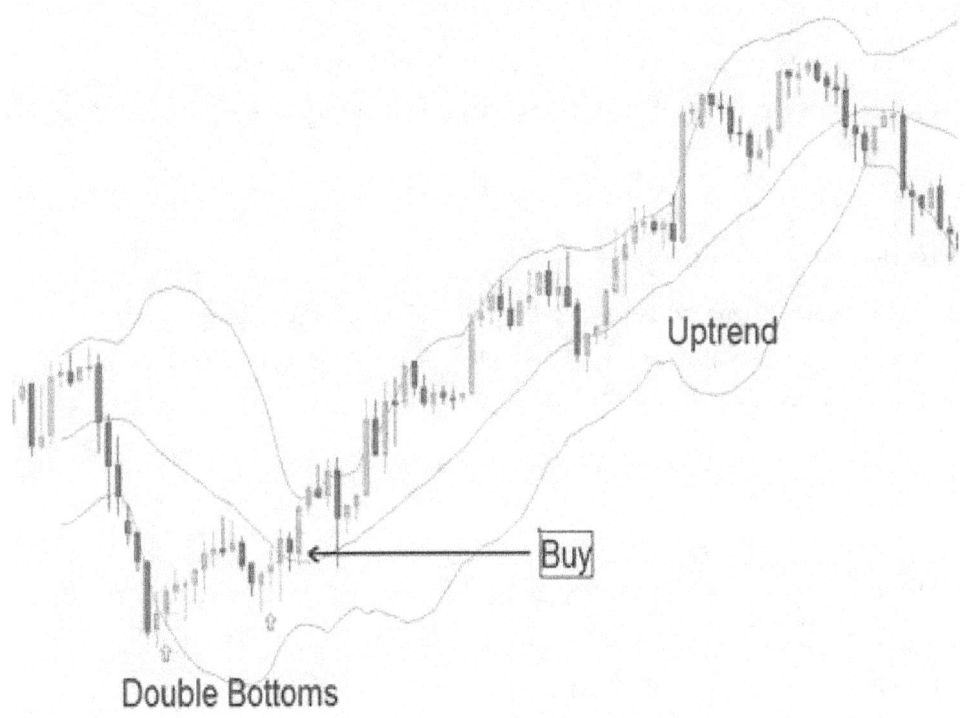

Psychological Support and Resistance

As market psychology underpins technical analysis, these simple methods can be very effective depending on the market traded.

Round numbers
52-week high and low

More hypothesis for the people who are intrigued. Go ahead and avoid this segment if you have any desire to zero in on commonsense use.

The many sorts of help and opposition recorded above could appear to be overpowering right away. Yet, you can arrange them in your psyche with these three spectra.

Reactive - Predictive

We distinguish responsive zones by seeing where cost has exchanged or where volume has concentrated, or both. The key here is that the S/R zones are checked in view of where the market has exchanged. We are responding to past market data.

Models incorporate swing turns (ups and downs), areas of blockage, cost holes.

For prescient zones, the market has not exchanged there, essentially not as of late. Thus, you can say that we foresee that the level will act as a S/R zone.

Models incorporate Fibonacci Augmentations, pattern lines, moving midpoints.

Static - Dynamic

A few types of help and opposition continue as before once stamped and are not refreshed. These are static zones. A model is an even zone projected from a swing turn.

There are likewise unadulterated powerful zones that are refreshed continually with every approaching cost tick. Most figured S/R zones (e.g., moving normal) fit the bill.

Some S/Rs lie some in the middle between and require occasional (or cost set off) refreshing. A pattern line refreshes with new swing turns. Floor broker turns utilized for day exchanging are reconsidered each exchanging meeting.

It's useful to be aware if your S/R zones are dynamic so you can guarantee that they are refreshed instantly, either physically or naturally.
Anticipated - Figured

Projected help and opposition depend completely on value elements and math. Subsequently, you can consider them being nearer to the basic cost activity.

Then again, figured S/R like moving midpoints are markers. A cost activity merchant will apply these instruments all the more judiciously.

Chapter 7

How to judge the significance of a support or resistance level

Analyzing the likelihood of a support or resistance area holding up is the crux to forming a trading strategy.

Try answering the following questions, and you will get a sense of how to perform such analysis.

How many times has the market touched the S/R?

There is a crucial trade-off here.

The more times the market tests the S/R, the more established the S/R becomes. If a zone is well-tested, we are more confident that the zone is indeed an S/R.

However, each time the market tests the S/R, it removes some of its potency.

For example, each time the market contacts a help level and skips up, it eliminates a few excited purchasers from that level. At last, with additional tests, there are not any more energetic purchasers at that level, and that is the point at which the help falls flat.

When the market does touch the S/R, how does the price action look like?

Each time the market touches the S/R, examine the price action closely for clues.

For instance, a healthy support zone will produce a vigorous bullish reaction to a test. Hence, if candlesticks with long lower shadows (like a Pin Bar reflecting buying pressure) form at a support zone, it's a positive signal.

Are there any decisive breaks of the S/R?

A decisive break refers to any price action formation that gives you the impression that the S/R is no longer effective.

Different traders identify decisive breaks differently. Here are some ideas:

A break beyond a certain ATR multiple (or other volatility measures)
A bar close beyond the S/R
A bar high below a support level or a bar low above a resistance level (my preference)
A swing low above a support level or a swing high below a resistance level

If there are decisive breaks, consider if the zone has flipped?
S/R flipping is a well-known concept.

A failed support becomes a proper resistance; a failed resistance becomes reliable
support.

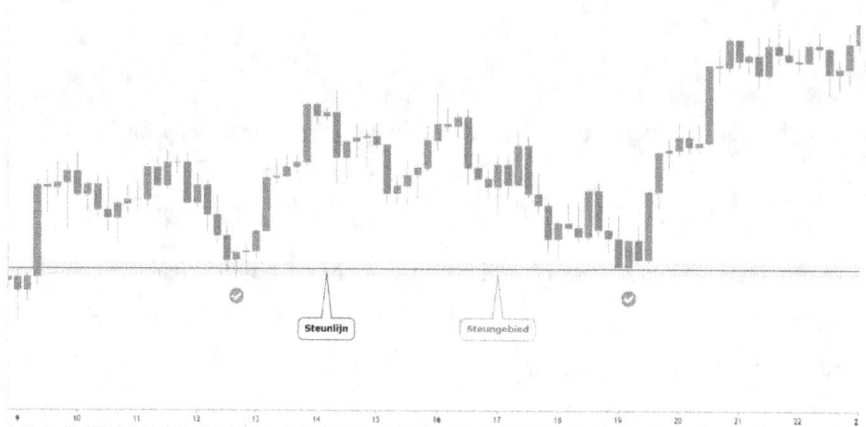

What time frame did the S/R originate from?

For the most part, the drawn out help and opposition zones recognized from bigger
time spans are more critical. This is useful in the event that you utilize numerous time
spans in your exchanging.

This perception shapes the premise of some various time span exchanging
methodologies.

Notwithstanding, the importance of the S/R time span to your exchanging skyline is
basic too. Also, that is the accompanying inquiry to address.

What is the relevance of the S/R compared to your trading horizon?

Think about that, from the week by week outline, you distinguished an unmistakable help zone, and you stamped it with certainty. Notwithstanding, that zone is not really pertinent to an intraday dealer examining the 3-minute outline.

The above is an outrageous guide to come to our meaningful conclusion.

By and by, you want to comprehend your exchanging technique well and amass sufficient experience to judge which S/Rs are useful to keep. Normally, think about the S/R's vicinity in time and cost to the ongoing business sector.

This is a fundamental inquiry since it assists you with keeping your graphs cleaned up. When you establish that a S/R is as of now not applicable, eliminate it from your graph.

Is there confluence?

Here, confluence refers to different methods producing S/R areas that overlap. If you find convergence, the zone is more likely to be reliable.

For instance, the intersection of a bear trend line and a horizontal resistance enjoys confluence. This is because both of them are potential resistance. The chart below shows this scenario.

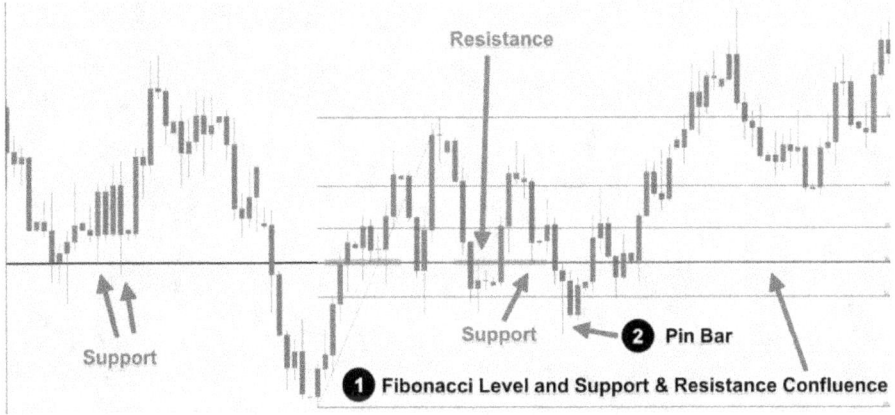

Confluence can also be a result of S/Rs found within different time frames. For instance, a weekly support zone coinciding with a daily support zone.

How to trade an S/R?

For a technical trader to enter a trade, we need to answer three questions:

How do you enter?

How do you exit if you are wrong?

How do you exit if you are correct?

Analyzing support and resistance can help to answer these questions. Their interplay is the premise of many trading strategies.

The process involves analyzing which S/Rs will hold up and which will break. We have covered the factors to consider in the last section.

For Entries

If you are confident of the support or resistance holding up, you can secure an optimal entry price with a limit order.

In this case, limit your risk with a volatility stop like the Chandelier Stops shown below.

If you need confirmation, look for price patterns at the S/R. In addition, the price patterns also offer pattern stops for controlling your risk.

The chart below shows such a scenario using the Anti-Climax pattern (marked with color arrows) at a support zone.

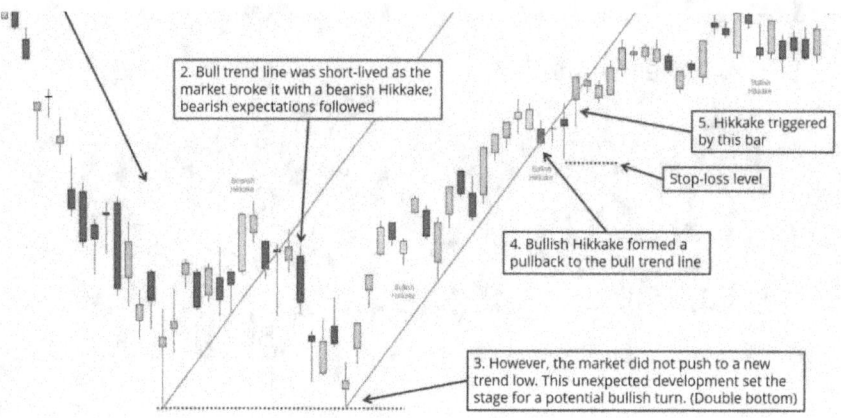

If you anticipate an S/R to hold, consider fading false breakouts. This approach can help you fine tune your entry and improve your reward-to-risk ratio. (To learn more, look into Wyckoff Upthrusts and Springs.)

The chart below shows a false breakout of a well-established support zone.

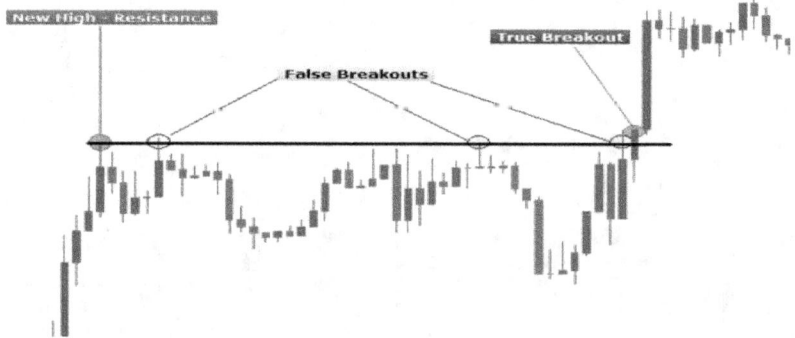

If you anticipate the S/R to fail, consider breakout pullbacks. While you can also trade breakouts directly, waiting for a retracement is more prudent.

The chart below shows two breakout pullbacks: one out of a bear trend line and another above the resistance zone.

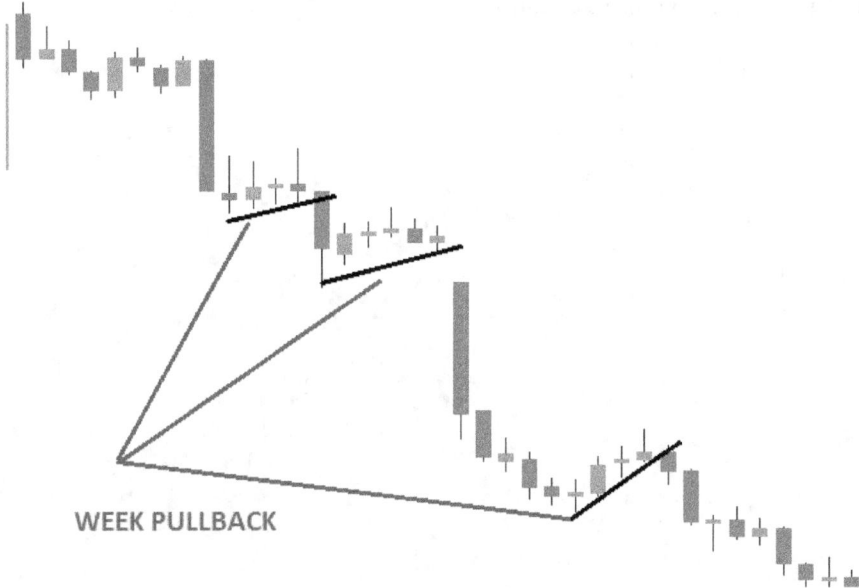

WEEK PULLBACK

For Taking Profits

You can use any reliable support and resistance to take profit.

As the market may be moving into a new area, you probably won't have responsive zones set apart out. Thus, prescient S/R procedures like Estimated Moves, Fibonacci Expansions, Pattern Line Channels may be more useful.

The graph underneath shows one of my #1 techniques for taking benefits, with a cost channel stretching out to a 200% line. You can take benefit at the 100 percent or 200% line, contingent upon your market evaluation.

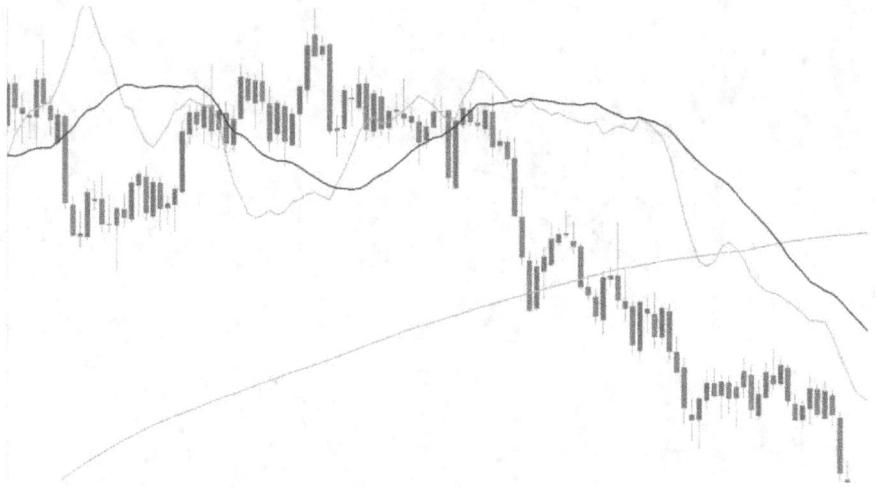

How to avoid potential pitfalls?

I cannot overstate the importance of having a consistent framework for marking support and resistance. Without such a framework, it's easy to fall victim to hindsight bias.

Adam Grimes did a simple experiment with random S/R levels to demonstrate how desperately our brains want to see patterns, even when they are none.

Building a consistent framework for S/R involves locking onto an objective method to define swing pivots. I use pure price action to do so in my course, but you can also use moving averages to help with that.

Also, keep things simple.

Resist the tendency to draw too many support and resistance levels. Too many zones lead to confusion. Try your best to identify the appropriate zones and remove the rest.

Market Bias

Market bias refers to the market's tendency to move in a particular direction, either up or down. You can also call it the market trend or price action context.

The market bias is what gives us our edge. It has a strong influence on the success of our trades, far more than any price pattern in isolation.

Market Bias Examples
To illustrate this point, we will look at how different patterns perform within a given market context.

The three charts below show the same set of price bars.

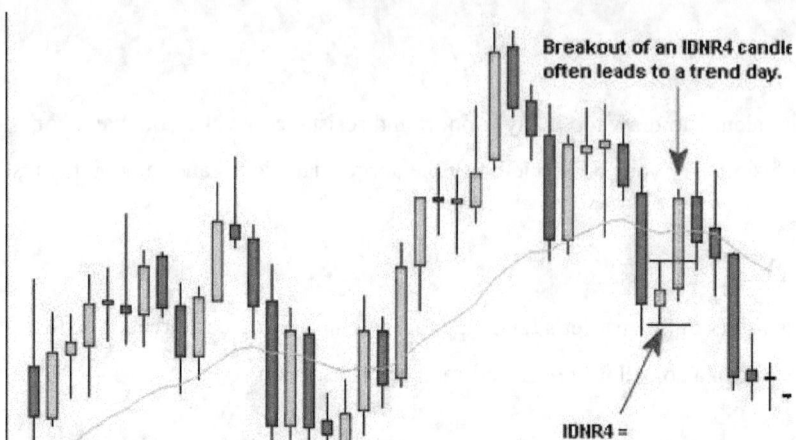

We also observed how Pin Bars performed in this market.

This last chart marks out the two-bar reversals.

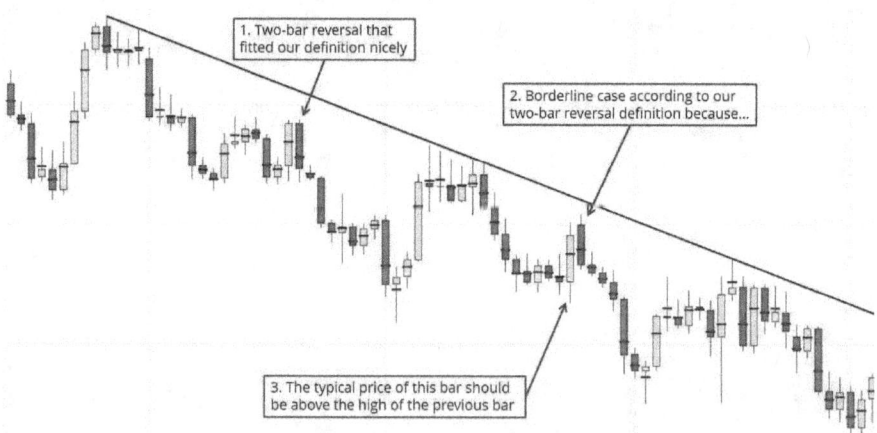

Conclusion

Price action is a simple trading strategy that helps traders with foreseeing market developments involving distinguished designs in the stock cost developments. Retail brokers, examiners, and arbitrageurs can follow this methodology for value expectations and hypothesis for a large number of monetary resources.

Price action is a simple trading strategy that helps traders with foreseeing market developments involving distinguished designs in the stock cost developments. Retail brokers, theorists, and arbitrageurs can follow this methodology for value expectations and theory for many monetary resources.

To begin with, cost activity is about effortlessness. Merchants need not swarm the cost graph with numerous specialized markers, such as moving midpoints, turn focuses, and so on. A mind boggling approach could cause pressure.

Second, exchanging choices in light of cost activity permit brokers to exchange ongoing, following business sector developments. It prompts lucidity that comprehends what precisely is going on the lookout. You can take a situation with certainty.

Third, time periods are critical in cost activity exchanging. Most dealers incline toward day to day and week by week time periods relying upon their inclination.

Fourth, signals made by cost activity are not difficult to get. You really want not be an expert in that frame of mind to comprehend cost activity.